INNER RUSTLINGS

Iqbal ismail Sait

(Ghalib sultan)

RIGI PUBLICATION

Inner Rustlings

By

Iqbal ismail Sait

Originally published in India

Edition:1

ISBN: 978-93-91041-35-9

Printer: Repro India

Published by RIGI PUBLICATION

777, Street no.9, Krishna Nagar Khanna-141401 (Punjab), India

Website: www.rigipublication.com

Email: info@rigipublication.com

Phone: +91-9357710014, +91-9465468291

POEMS

1.	DE – EVOLUTION	5
2.	DEATH OF AN 'ALIEN KIND'	7
3.	"I SEE MY GOD"----- "I SAY OH ! MY GOD"	8
4.	'DREAMS AND ------ ALL DREAMS'	14
5.	'MEANINGS' --- IF ANY ?	15
6.	PLANET 'Z' –A DISTANT HOPE	17
7.	'YEARNINGS'	19
8.	'A PERFECT HUMAN BEING'	20
9.	DAWN	21
10.	'GREATNESS'	23
11.	' MANNA' OF MAMMOTH RUINS	24
12.	GONE FOREVER	30
13.	'MOTHERS'----THEY ALL	31
14.	REMEMBERING THE 'LADY WITH THE LAMP'	33
15.	'PARADISE' TO 'HELL'	35
16.	'BEAUTY' AND 'THE BEAST'	37
17.	THE ONLY 'HOPE'	39
18.	'ENDANGERED SPECIES' . . . ADDING A 'HUMANSPECIES'	41
19	'HEAVEN' IS TOO CLOSE TO 'HELL'!	43
20.	'LITTLE DROPS OF WATER MAKE THE MIGHTY OCEAN'	44
21.	THE THRUST OF 'I' IN ME	46
22.	'THE CELL'	47
23.	'HAPPINESS'----PURCHASEABLE?	49
24.	STARTED 'THE COUNTDOWN'	50
25.	VANISHING A 'PAST ELIXIR'	52
26.	'THE AFTERMATH'	53

27.	ONLY 'THE NUMBER' THAT COUNTS	55
28.	'ALFA, BETA, DELTA, OMICRON - - - - -'	56
29.	'DEM(ON)OCRACY'	57
30.	'MEMORIES'- - - - FASTER THAN LIGHT ?	58
31.	EQUALITY	59
32.	'MATTER - OF – FACTNESS'	61
33.	IN THE NAME OF THE 'MOST MERCIIFUL---'	62
34.	INSTANT REVIVAL OF A 'GOLDEN' PAST	63
35.	'MIRAGE'	64
36.	EXISTENCE	65
37.	MUCH MORE THAN 'EQUALS'	66
38.	'HOLOCAUST' - PERSONIFIED	67

DE – EVOLUTION

It all started, no one really knows when.
Or hasn't it been there all the time ?
Or hasn't even Time started then ?
Or from it came the beginning of Time ?
With it began the timeless beginning,
And followed it the beginning of everything.

Not knowing the Past and uncertain of the Future,
All started to take forms and formless forms.
Meanings and purposes had to be there; it was sure;
Or else how could there be, among the vast forms
An Order of some form ? the Question to all is so clear.

Answer has to come from the Starting Point
Of an Endless Tunnel and the sheer
Distance makes the Question itself quaint.
No light of knowledge could travel back that far,
Nor could it travel farther ahead,
So as to know things to come for sure.
Whether fairness to some, the Order provided,
And to others unfairness
Purpose to some and void to others,
Justice to some and to many injustice,
Is the glaring moot Question

If with the beginning
There existed an Order
Then why the Omnipotent
That created the Order
Wanted, after many many
Millenniums,even
Many milleniums after
The appearance of human being
So many religions that
Are Fighting each other ?

When the Order is Sublime
And its Creator the most Sublime
Why many Religions ?
Instead of one ?

The Question is so enthralling that
The Theologian, the Philosopher,
The Scientist, even the Politician
All have started answering.
In Affirmation, in Negation,
Or in sheer Confusion, in degrees of variation.
Lo - still survives the Layman in all this Murky Mist.

DEATH OF AN 'ALIEN KIND'

All life springs up from its `death'.
The 'death' that started the moment it was born.
All die when it stops 'dying'
And becomes absolutely dead.
Turning itself into molten ash,
Burning, not living a moment,
Dying every second;
The SUN never fails to die
Till it is dead indeed.

"I SEE MY GOD"----- "I SAY OH ! MY GOD"

On a holiday, seeing
A pleasantly cool bright day
I decide to take a long walk.

Walking some distance, leaving
My small town behind,
I enter a wilderness, adjacent to my town.

Walking through the wilderness,
Enjoying the freshness of Nature
I suddenly spot a flock of flamingoes at a distance
I approach them silently and watch them
Dancing with measured steps,
Keeping their beautifully coloured wings wide open,
Repeating certain steps exactly
With the same timings as before;
As if not to take a wrong step
In disharmony with the Music
They alone can hear.
'I see My God'

Turning fom them, walking farther,
All of a sudden all the colours in the world
Come to my sight.
With the breeze bringing a fragrance, that is

So sweet and special, it goes
Straight into my heart.
The flowers in so many different
Hues and colours in all shapes
And sizes are all dancing
In the caressing breeze.
‘ I see My God ‘

Walking deeper into the widerness,
The Great Artist spell binds me
In yet another way.

Again colours are fluttering
Above my head---- helter skelter.
Some of them begin to settle down
On flowers and leaves around me
And started displaying the magnificent
Art work depicted on them by
Moving their wings slowly up and down.

The butterflies simply marvel me
With the exquisite, symmetrical
And wonderfully beautiful
Designs and colours imprinted
On their wings.
‘I see My God’

Walking back home, I notice
The recently opened Portrait Art Gallery
Of a renowned Artist of my Town.

Entering the Gallery I find
Portraits of great personalities of all time.
Isaac Newton, Albert Einstein,
William Shakespeare, Mozart, Beethoven
Mahatma Gandhi, Mother Teresa, Michael Angelo so on so forth.

Those were remarkably
So well portrayed that I feel
As if I were standing in front of
The live persons in the pictures.

In all those persons
In the portraits
And In the Great Artist
Who has created them- - - - -
'I see My God'

Falling back to the routine life - - - - -
I wake up next day morning
Picking up the newspaper
With a cup of tea in my hand
I am taken aback when I see
Photographs of a school bus,

Laying upside down, half
Submerged in water and
Those of a number of
Kindergarten children
Who made their last journey
In that fateful bus which
Went over the side rails of a bridge- - -- - -
'I say Oh! My God'

Proceeding to my Office in my car,
Stopped at the traffic Red Signal,
Waiting 70 seconds for the Green to come in
I look around to see the street sights of our Metro City.
Giant hoardings of jewellery, textiles,villas
All casting long shadows on one side of the street.

Underneath those Mega structures
My eyes catch movements of an object
That is moving towards the stalled traffiic.
Coming coser to my car
I find a boy of about 8,
Sitting on a wooden plank
On small wheels, pushing the plank with one hand.

Reaching close to my car
I find his other hand below the shoulder
And his both legs below the knees

Crippled and wasted,
He was extending his only hand towards me.
As the Green comes in
Non stop honking horns
From vehicles behind me
Push my car forward
I throw whatever I have
In my pocket into his hands
Driving the car forward
My lips murmured - - - - - -
'Oh! My God'

After office hours I return home;
Taking a relaxing bath,
I try to unwind myself.
Switching, on the T V I go for
Old songs slotted at that time.
After listening to the Divine
Voice of Rafi Saheb,
That takes me to a different world
I switch on to the News channel

My day is not to end peacefully.
Coming on the screen I see debris of
Collapsed buildings and
Scattered peices of human bodies.

Breaking News------
------Multiple bombs in a Mall
So far have killed 48 innocent people
In a western European City,
And the people who have done it,
Identifying themselves have
Proudly taken credit of it-----
'I say Oh ! My God'
Yes 'I see My God' and 'I say Oh ! My God'
Yet I really crave to say 'I see my God' always.

‘DREAMS AND ------ ALL DREAMS’

Dreams come to you while you sleep
You have little say over dreams while you sleep
But you can dream your Future
While you are awake

As you become conscious of your Living world
You start dreaming the Immediate Future
As you grow up you never stop dreaming your Future
These are the Dreams keep you moving.

All your Dreams about the Future
Remain as dreams until they take shapes
How they turn out to be make you what you are.

'MEANINGS' --- IF ANY ?

Honesty, Integrity, determination
Love, affection, empathy- -   - - -

Names of Virtues and values
Can go on and on

An infant entering childhood
Learning Virtues and Values
Tries hard to adopt them
In his small world

Working hard, never letting down
The Virtues and Values he learnt
He reaches his adulthood

Facing the Real World
He starts doubting the relevance
Of his Vitues and Values
In his Daily Life
His zest and vigour begin to fade

Past adulthood, entering middle age
He slowly learns to attribute
Meanings of Virtues and Values
According to the Context and Circumstances

Considering SUCCESS as the only
Goal in life, he now gives
Appropriate meanings to
Virtues and Values to acheive
That SUCCESS

And finally nearing his last days
He thinks he has acheived
The SUCCESS he wanted- - -
But always with a lingering
Pricking deep in his heart

PLANET 'Z' –A DISTANT HOPE

Planet 'Z' was discovered 6 years ago
As the most habitable planet
Outside Mother Earth

Few sponsors soon started
To offer 'package deals'
For migration and for arranging
Complete settlement on the planet
Inviting advance registration
For the Space Shuttle travels

Since then there had been
Heavy rush of Super Riches to 'Planet Z'
Those who have landed
Find themselves in a Heavenly World;
Air is pure and clean
Water is crystal clear

Beautifully built residences
And entirely completed infrastructure works,
No traffic jam no pollution.

Government elected from
The Z inhabitants
Takes care of everything

Activities of production and manufacture
Do not contaminate air or water
No corruption or bribe yet
It is Paradise itself.

Only one Dilemma !
That too very big Dilemma !

Whom should they address as God ?
So far all Gods originated
From Earthbound religions

Now they are in Planet Z
With the next generation
Any link with earth
Would be removed.

Few wise men told them
Do not place God within
The frameworks of religion
Let religion be built around
The Omnipresent God

Then there cannot be many
But one religion
How many of them did
Realise the difference ?
Anybody's guess.

'YEARNINGS'

Why are you yearning for what is NOT ?
Why are you craving for what CAN NEVER BE ?
Why dont you become rational?
Why dont you become sensible ?
Why dont you become realistic ?
Why dont you become practical?

You tell me I am irrational and insensible
You tell me I am not realistic
You tell me I am not practical

I can be only what I am
I cannot become anybody else
My yearnings are for a world of love and justice
My yearnings are for responsible freedom for all

If I become such a rational, sensible
Realistic and practical person
Then you would be looking at a man of your choice

I would not be there any more

'A PERFECT HUMAN BEING'

Happiness or sadness
Anger or depression
Pride or envy
Anxiety or complacency
Love or hatred

Nothing should bother him !
He wants to be insulated from all these
He doesn't want to be a Victim of any Emotion.

So you may think he wants to become a Rishi ?
Or you may think he wants to become a Super Human?
Or you may even think he is sub human ? or inhuman ?
Nothing of the sort !
He wants to be a Perfect Human being

Human being has larger brains
Compared to other living beings
His reasoning is much superior to theirs
All his Emotions have no direct links
To his Wellbeing and Progress
He doesn't want to become a Victim of any Emotion
He just wants to become a Perfect Human being.

DAWN

Getting up very early in the morning
I found the Forest Resort where I was staying
In stony silence and darkness

After finishing my morning ritual
I stepped out of my cottage into the yard
And walked towards
The thick growth of trees and plants

Very soft and gentle breeze
Caressing my face
With untainted, unique
Smell of Mother Earth and
The surrounding foliage

I saw the pre-dawn light
In the big gap between two groups of trees
Where the land seems to touch the sky.

I stood frozen watching
The unmatched glory
Of a rising sun.

With the accompaniment music
Of chirping birds

The emerging Sun
Dispells darkness in
Every second of its ascendance
As if to give new Hopes
To the World below

Not grasping the message
The World below
Still sleeps on and on------

'GREATNESS'

People say he is Great - - -
Is it achieved by him?
Or thrust upon him?
Or claimed by him?
Or Is he born Great?

Well ! never mind the distinction
He is simply Great
As long as people say he is.

With so many Great men
And women around
One has to tread cautiously
Lest he falls to the pit
Of some Greatness or other

Once he becomes Great
The whole world is changed
His world would be
What people would assign to him

So one has to be extra cautious !

' MANNA' OF MAMMOTH RUINS

No; they must not miss the onset of
The much fancied Kerala Monsoon.
The decision was unanimous.
They have planned everything
Very well in advance

They have reserved flight tickets
To Cochin and back to Delhi
And accommodation in a
Small hill top Resort in Kerala

David, Imran, and Rajeev,
Classmates, for years, from school to college
Got the approval of their parents much early

So started their journey to God's own Country

As the aircraft started descending,
The glorious sight of very picturesque
Kerala came to their view

The bright evening sun spread
It's blanket of golden rays
Over the mountains and lakes

The mountains, the lush greenery,
The lakes, like golden ribbons,
Were all so enchanting that
They forgot about the Monsoon

After checking into the Resort
Rajeev asked the Manager
'When will the Monsoon start?'

'Anytime now'
Was the reply

The next day morning
They were woken up
By the sound of raindrops
Slashing the window panes.
They jumped up with joy
To watch the arrival of Kerala Monsoon.

At the breakfast table,the Delhi lads
Were joined by two other guests.
The Manager the Cook and a staff
Stood in attendance near the table.

Rain intensified; all the guests
Decided to remain indoors
And enjoy watching the rain.

After all, they all have come
Just for this purpose.

Enjoy; they really did.

Afternoon TV Channels
Started showing many
Parts of Kerala getting flooded.

By evening rain further intensified

Now the Boys started showing concerns
Still the message they
Sent back home was
'They all were enjoying Mansoon'

They went to bed
With uneasy minds
It was raining without break.

Rajeev was the first one
To get up around 5 am
Through the window,
In the dim light,
He saw the yard filled
With knee deep water
He pulled up David and Imran

It was still raining heavily.
Intense fear was clearly
Writ on the lads' faces.

They rushed to the Manager
For getting some conveyance
To get to a safer place

'It is dead' said the Manager
Pointing to the telephone
Switching on his mobile
He started shouting to someone

Then turning to the lads,
Almost, breathless, words
Tumbled out of his mouth- - - -
" I have asked for a Rescue Boat- - - -
the whole place is flooded "

The Manager with trembling fingers
Switched on the TV News
Pictures of heavily flooded areas
With up rooted trees and destroyed
Buildings appeared on the screen.

The death toll reported was 230.

A frantic David dragging
His friends along, rushed to the door
Screaming "We will swim and
Reach safety"

"Don't do foolish thing" shouted the Manager
"This Resort is at a higher level- - - -
and all the places below would have drowned- - -
and you too would be drowned- - --
if the rain ceases or the boat comes- - -
you have better chances"

They were all in shell shock
And started praying for
The rain to stop and the boat to come.

The rain did not stop.
The boat did not come.

By afternoon the electricity went off.

Then all the mobiles gone dead.

They could hear the gurgles of water
Outside the door.
They could feel the pressure
Of some great force on the walls.

By late evening darkness gathered
Inside the Resort.

They put heavy objects behind
The closed doors and windows.

The low sound of their moans
Filled the air of the tightly closed Resort.

The tick tock of the wall clock
Pounded their hearts heavily.

Suddenly a mountain of water,
Crashing down the side wall
And half of the roof,
Fell on their heads,
Burying them under the debris.

Two days later the Emergency
Flood help Office started
Getting a flurry of calls
From Delhi asking the
Whereabouts of David, Imran , and Rajeev.

Another two days later
'Not traceable'
Was the reply sent back.

GONE FOREVER

Every Second
Once gone, gone forever

No matter whatever
You try to recreate
That Moment, it won't be
The same again- - -
----good or bad !!

The fleeing Second
Carries away
Everything
In it forever !

Hardly anyone is
Aware of it !

'MOTHERS'----THEY ALL

A Cheetah facing aLion
To save her baby!

A Rat biting the tail
Of an attacking snake
To save her baby!

An Elephant stands
Close to her dead baby
For days on end

Watching all this on TV,
I wonder any Bondage
More intense than
Of a Mother to her child.

Looking around
Our own world
I find I am wrong!

Dead babies are found
In canals and ditches
Babies are thrown away
to the sea.

Many are the ways
Some ‘ Mothers ‘ discard
Their babies!!

What a “ Progress “
Homosapiens have made!!

Yes , ‘Mothers’ ----they all.

REMEMBERING THE 'LADY WITH THE LAMP'

How can one ever forget her?
--- Florence Nightingale,
The 'Lady with the Lamp'

She was the synonym of
Sympathy, empathy
And devotion.

Coming to recent times,
How can one forget
The' Lady with the Cyanide'?

She is the personification of
Evil and Deceit

She has schemed
And killed several
Of her own kith and kin;
Patiently timing
The killings over some years!!

She is the most infamous woman
Of Gods Own country, Kerala.

How can one fathom
The psyche of these two extreme
Characters?
Then, how can one ever attempt
To unravel all the Mysteries
Of the Universe that has
Bright shining stars
As well as deep, dark Black Holes?

‘PARADISE’ TO ‘HELL’

Travel back in Time,
Travel back decades,
Carry your memories along;
You reach Paradise on Earth
----you reach Kashmir

The fragrance of flowers,
Serene, silent Dal Lake,
Snow capped mountains---
All welcome you heartily.

Healthy happy men and women
Embrace you with their
Warmth and Hospitality.

Travel back decades to Kashmir
And you sit by the shore of the Dal Lake,
Watching Kashmiris
In their colourful dresses
Rowing the House Boats;
Some singing their traditional songs
And hundreds of tourists
Keeping the rhythm
By clapping their hands.
All these are things of the Past.

Coming to the Present
You are dumbfounded with Horror
Hardly a day passes
Without blood bath.

In this blind, senseless, endless
Tussle a Paradise on Earth
Is simply disappearing.

'BEAUTY' AND 'THE BEAST'

The slowly flowing river,
The snow capped mountains
ALL turn into gold
As the setting Sun spreads
Its golden rays all over.

I sit all alone in that
Completely silent valley
Disturbed only by
Occasional bird calls.

Earthy fragrance
Envelops me all over.

----I am thrown into
A Dream World

As darkness gradually
Gathers, the sky, yonder
The mountain tops,
Began to lighten up.

Within minutes I become
Motionless; staring
At the super bright
And large full Moon.

The snow tops of the mountains
Become blazingly white,
The whole river slowly
Turns into a large, wavy,
Reflecting Silver sheet.

Indeed an unmatched
Display of Nature's
Exotic Beauty!

But when, world over,
A Beast assumes
The forms of
Development and Progress
----and when Nature itself
Starts vanishing---------
------and when an angry
Greta Thunberg made an outburst
At the Powers that might be
"You have stolen my Dreams,
----what right you have got to destroy
This 'Beautiful World' ?

----crying hoarse, I repeat
Her Question million times.

THE ONLY 'HOPE'

How come so many
Similar happenings
Occur in their lives?
Wonder these two Bosom friends !

Both studied together
Both passed out
With high Distinctions.

Both had acclaimed
Top most achievements
And were honored
With the highest awards
Of the Nation

--- but that was long, long time back

Even today very similar
Are their plights of life !

Poverty started holding
Its nasty grip tighter and tighter
On them both

No letters, nor calls
Which were flowing in
In their Glorious Days.

Both the aging friends
Struggle hard to make
Both ends meet

Hard days pass by;
One day one bosom
Friend dies

Rushing to the Funeral
Are Ministers, VVIPs.
Rich tributes Paid
Heavy cash endowments
Announced to the family

Returning from
The Funeral, the thought
In the mind of
The living friend was- - - -
- - - the 'Only Hope is Death'

'ENDANGERED SPECIES' .... ADDING A 'HUMANSPECIES'

Another day is dying out
---So are the few souls
In that Old Age Home.

They have assembled
In the Court Yard, as usual
They do in the evenings.

There are Couples and
There are Singletons.

They all have reached
Their Dusky Days.

The Couples meet
Their Mates only
In the evenings.

Singletons struggle
To find companions.

For all of them
The constant companions
Of their long, lonely hours
Are the memories of their children.

Children who used to
Run upto tem for anything
And everything
----now too grown up
To pay a visit to them.

With Gay marriages, Lesbianism
And co-habitation becoming
The order of the Day,
Biologists are on the verge of
Declaring as ‘ Endangered’
A Human Species called
‘PARENTS’

'HEAVEN' IS TOO CLOSE TO 'HELL'!

Why this uneasiness?
Why this restlessness?

He just cannot find
Any reason for his
Own pathetic state.

Alas, he is in Heaven;
In the midst of unimaginable,
Exquisite Pleasures.

Why then this haunting
Feeling of some impending
Disaster?

Suddenly it dawned on him---
Though he is in the lap of Pleasures,
How long can he live in Heaven
Without breaking its
Stringent Rules?

Once the Rules broken
He, no doubt, would be
In the Next Door Hell !!

'LITTLE DROPS OF WATER MAKE THE MIGHTY OCEAN'

Sitting in the balcony
Of the Cruise ship,
Watching- - -
The sheer Enormity,
The sheer Vastness,
The sheer Magnetism,
The sheer Presence itself
Of the Mighty Ocean
I become transfixed.

It spreads over the entire
Field of Vision; as if to stress
The insignificance
Of the land it faces
---and its inhabitants.

Watching the wavy
Surface of this boundless,
Blue- green carpet;
I wonder at the whopping,
Gigantic Force, Power
And Mass that lay hidden
Underneath this seemingly
Innocent Carpet !!

If it turns really wild
And makes an Angry Surge
The land and its inhabitants
Would simply vanish
In NO TIME.

THE THRUST OF 'I' IN ME

How can 'I' be a Cog
In the Machine ?
How can 'I' be taken
For granted ?

I must make use of
My abilities to enjoy
Life's comforts and pleasures
As best as possible

If I don't, no doubt,
A Fool I would be

Nothing should detract
Me from achieving my Goal.
My Relations, Friends,
Home and Home Town
All must fall within
The Limits of my Goal;
If they don't, let them be
Out of my World.

Yes, I am aware
In my last Days
I would be left with
None but MYSELF.

'THE CELL'

So convenient, so compact
And less bothersome
Is ' The Cell '.

'The Cell' makes you
More focused, efficient
And productive.

'The Cell' brings out
Your potentials
And makes your
Presence Distinct.

Yes, The Cell family
Is more visible,
More recognized.

Yet, in ' The Cell ' you
Miss out certain elements
That are deeply rooted inside you.

They are the elements of
Your Bondage with
The people you took
Your origin from.

These missing elements
Leave a lurking pain
Deep in your heart.

'HAPPINESS'----PURCHASEABLE?

Purchasing power matters.
If one has the purchasing power,
Why shy away from
Purchasing Happiness?

But then, this alone,
May not produce Happiness;
One has to deliberately
Switch on to the Happiness mode.

Otherwise, a waste of
Money and time.
One shouldn't forget
The money paid.

So switch on to the Happiness mode.
---then its all one's Luck!

STARTED 'THE COUNTDOWN'

Science says our dear Earth
Came into existence
Billions of years ago,
Nine Billion years
After the Big Bang,
That set in motion
The Act of Creation.

Science goes on to say
We, the Homosapiens
Emerged less than
Three million years ago.

The All Powerful Homosapiens
Have this planet at their disposal.

They are bent upon making
Progress, Gains and Success
At whatever cost- - -
They never mind

The result is getting
More and more evident.

For our dear Earth,
Having passed Billions of years,
Now started THE COUNTDOWN
--- may be for the last few hundreds!!

VANISHING A 'PAST ELIXIR'

Traditions, Culture, Prosperity
And even Civilizations
Do generate on the banks of
An ever flowing , lush river.

Such a river was , once,
This body of water
That is spread out
In front of me.

The scattered rocks and
The patches of sand,
Visible above the water surface,
Like the protruding ribs
Of a hunger struck man,
Are crying out
The pathetic state of
The motionless water,
Which was, once,
A Great River called
'Bharatha Puzha'

'THE AFTERMATH'

The dawn of year 2020
Marked the beginning of
A Disaster, the like of
Which, the World has
Never seen before.

Nations become still,
Hospitals get crowded,
Death toll rises by the day;
The Virus Corona marches on.

Within days the onslaught
Becomes a Global Phenomenon;
And the Virus establishes itself
As an unstoppable Conqueror,
Taking the lives of thousands on its way.

Hustles and Bustles of
The Markets fade out,
Economies of all Nations
Take nosedives.
Unemployment and poverty
Stare at millions of people.

Scientists in the Labs
Crack their brains
To find a Vaccine,
The only Hope, that
Could Arrest the spread.
Politicians at the Top
Who could have done much
To arrest the spread,
Are now after the Scientists
To get a Vaccine within
No time, as if to get it
Out of thin air!!

Writing on the wall is clear;
The Virus Corona is here to stay
For days and days and days- - - - -
With its power of Lethal Strike,
Which may or may not prove
As 'Ominous' as it has been.

ONLY 'THE NUMBER' THAT COUNTS

Constitution? Justice? Legality?
Leave them aside when ' the Number' counts.

Evidences after evidences?
So what? Can they overcome
The number of Votes- - -
---when it matters?

If you have 'the Number' with you
No need to shut your Big Mouth---
---no need to stop tweeting;

Just spill out and type out
Anything you want----
----just go on and on----

So teaches the Head of the
Most powerful Nation in the World!

Never mind----
Constitution, Justice, Legality----

'ALFA, BETA, DELTA, OMICRON - - - - -'

Whatever shape or form they come,
No Problem; we will name them.

What if they go on thriving,
We, the Scientists know their structures;
And identify them by names.

Our only problem is to keep
Names ready for the ever evolving Corona !

'DEM(ON)OCRACY'

'For the people'
'By the people'

But mostly for
'By the people'

For the 'people' who
Govern the 'real people'

Freedom of speech
Guarantees no bar
On the repeated lies
They dish out to
The 'real people'.

And lies are accepted
As a matter of course!

In Dem(on)ocracy
Judiciary is so 'efficient'
That a case seldom
Gets over in one's life time!

'MEMORIES'- - - - FASTER THAN LIGHT ?

Anything travels faster than Light?
Nothing known so far

If anything can,
It can travel even to the Past!
Even upto the Big Bang!

But to travel to the Past,
Your Memories can take you
Upto their limits,
Like, Kintergarten days
Or to the days of your childhood
Or to the days of your youth
In a fraction of a second;
No matter how old you are!

Yes, Memories do trancend
Even the speed of Light!

EQUALITY

'Equality' among All;
Can be achieved
By distributing Wealth
And Facilities equally to All?

But then can All be made
To act and think alike ?

With different circumstances
And surroundings and with
Varying Brain Capacities,
All can never think and act alike.

Most of the 'Brainy ones' or
'Intellectuals' would grab more than
What is given to them as 'equals' by
Using their higher thinking capabilities.

One may call it the "Law of Nature"

If ' Equality among All ' to be made
Literally practical, in every sense
Of the word, then, Humans have to be
Produced in Labs, with strict,
Uniform specifications !

If no one is deprived of, not only
Basic Needs, but all other needs
For leading a Decent Life
In the Modern World, then
If some get some things
More than others, wont it be
Desireable to leave it
As the " Law of Nature" ?

‘MATTER - OF – FACTNESS’

When the fact of the matter
Is known to you,
That is what it matters.

Why you think about
Anything else?

Yes, Prosaic they are
And never they go astray

And finally they pass away
Without getting a glimpse
Of the Spelendour
Of this Beautiful world!

IN THE NAME OF THE 'MOST MERCIIFUL---'

Yes we execute and remove
All those who do not think
And act as we wish them to do.

We have to do this
In the name of the Most Merciful
And the Benevolent.
It is His wish we carry out.
We see to it that no one disobeys.

The terrified Afghans
Tried to flee, risking
Their own lives
From the clutches of the Fanatics.

Their flight was so desperate,
That they tried to cling on to Death itself,
By hanging to the bottom of a fast moving
Aircraft that was about to take off.

And Death did embrace them.
They had attained Salvation;
When they reached a place
Where no one can execute them.

INSTANT REVIVAL OF A 'GOLDEN' PAST

Getting down from my car
To the busy street, an old lady caught
my attention.

Some remarkable familiariarity
In her face stopped me.

Took only few moments;
Yes, yes she is my History Teacher!

History Teacher in my school;
Several decades ago.

Though with some trepidation,
I approached her.

Do you remember me? I ask
Looking at me intently few moments,
Herr eyes sparkled.

Is it you- - - - - -?
From then flowed memories
Of those days, when Affinity
And Affection existed
Above Cast or Religion.

'MIRAGE'

Many centuries ago,
Centuries before the
Birth of christ,
Socrates, Plato and
Followers Struggled
Hard to up hold
'Justice' over 'Injustice'

There had been strong
Proponents of Injustice
Like Thrasymachus,
Whom Socrates and Plato
Had to contend with

Thrasymachus argued
That the stronger will
Continue to dictate terms,
Mostly in ' Unjust' manner.

'Justice' – a 'Mirage'
And will that remain
As such forever?

EXISTENCE

Once born, till dead,
One has to go through
The 'Time of one's Existence'.

Each and everyone
Travels through this 'Time'
Every different way.

And completes his journey
Every different way.

For some, the 'Time of Existence'
Provides moments of glory,
For some others it provides
Moments of mediocrity,
For still others moments of despair.

And yet for others
Nothing but moments of agony !!

MUCH MORE THAN 'EQUALS'

Homosapiens are
No Match for them.
They are Superior
By all means.

With the rapid, fast
Improvements in their intellect
The Chimpanzees simply
Outdo and outsmart humans !

Humans simply become
Inferior and servile
To Chimpanzees to the
Extent that they are
Kept in cages in some zoos,

----they even become
Cherished delicacy
In the Great Ape's Menu!!

Well, the Scenario
Could have been a Reality
Had some of the elements
Of the Evolution developed
A little differently!!!

'HOLOCAUST' - PERSONIFIED

Come what may,
I will get what I want.

Till then nothing, yes,
Nothing can stop me.

Death, agonies and sufferings
Of millions - - nothing
Can come in my way.

And I know fully well
The foolish World
Will simply look on
As I march towards
My destination.

So the Russian marches on;
And the World looks on;
Remains mute, watching the Holocaust !!

www.ingramcontent.com/pod-product-compliance
Lightning Source LLC
LaVergne TN
LVHW090135160826
845673LV00017B/2478

* 9 7 8 9 3 9 1 0 4 1 3 5 9 *